The Gospel according to
Harry Potter

The Gospel according to Harry Potter

Leader's Guide for Group Study

Connie Neal
and Samuel F. (Skip) Parvin

WESTMINSTER
JOHN KNOX PRESS
LOUISVILLE · KENTUCKY

Scripture quotations, unless otherwise indicated, are from the New Revised Standard Version of the Bible, copyright © 1989 by the Division of Christian Education of the National Council of the Churches of Christ in the U.S.A., and used by permission.

Scripture quotations marked NEB are taken from *The New English Bible,* © The Delegates of the Oxford University Press and The Syndics of the Cambridge Univeristy Press, 1961, 1970. Used by permission.

Book design by Sharon Adams

First edition
Published by Westminster John Knox Press
Louisville, Kentucky

This book is printed on acid-free paper that meets the American National Standards Institute Z39.48 standard. ∞

PRINTED IN THE UNITED STATES OF AMERICA

04 05 06 07 08 09 10 11 12 13 — 10 9 8 7 6 5 4 3 2

Library of Congress Cataloging-in-Publication Data

Neal, C. W. (Connie W.), 1958–
    The gospel according to Harry Potter : leader's guide for group study / Connie Neal and Samuel F. (Skip) Parvin.— 1st ed.
        p. cm.
    ISBN 0-664-22669-8 (alk. paper)
    1. Rowling, J. K.—Religion. 2. Rowling, J. K.—Study and teaching. 3. Children—Books and reading—English-speaking countries. 4. Christian fiction, English—Study and teaching. 5. Children's stories, English—Study and teaching. 6. Fantasy fiction, English—Study and teaching. 7. Rowling, J. K.—Characters—Harry Potter. 8. Potter, Harry (Fictitious character). 9. Spirituality in literature. 10. Religion in literature. I. Parvin, Samuel F., 1953– II. Title.

    PR6068.O93Z777 2004
    823'.914—dc21

                                                                        2003053771

Contents

Foreword

The greatest joy I found from reading the Harry Potter stories went beyond enjoying the stories themselves. It had everything to do with *sharing* the stories as we read them aloud together as a family, then added the friends who came to join us. The group's excited speculation about what might come next, who could be trusted, how the characters would overcome the dangers, whether or not those characters we grew to despise would get what was coming to them, and so on was a large part of the pleasure of reading. The discussions enriched our reading—as long as we did not pause too long in the middle of a chapter. Together we discussed: What might we have missed that will be revealed before we guess? What might we have presumed would turn out to be very different? And around our house, What elements of these fantasy stories would be forbidden by God in our real world? With our family, reading a book or watching a movie, a musical, or dramatic play tends to naturally flow into Bible discussions. (We have been doing this since our children were old enough to talk.)

When I wrote *The Gospel according to Harry Potter*, I hoped others would enjoy a similar shared group experience. Therefore, I am grateful to all who have worked together to create this study guide and to you as group leader or participant. I wrote *The Gospel according to Harry Potter* a bit tongue-in-cheek. "Oh, you see *witchcraft?* You're kidding, right? I see the Christian gospel all the way through!" Indeed, that was my perception (probably because I seek such parallels in everything), but I never intended my perceptions to be a declarative statement on *the* gospel as found in the Harry Potter stories. Rather, my aim was to get people to think outside the cauldron, to spark conversation and provoke thought so that others might share the joy of considering the "glimmers of the gospel" they *might* find there—if they went in looking for that rather than looking for witchcraft (as some Christians have chosen to do).

Therefore, I am delighted to see such beginnings being further developed, illuminated, and expanded through the expertise of Skip Parvin, coauthor of *The Gospel according to The Simpsons: Leader's Guide for Group Study* and an established writer of youth curriculum and editor and writer for *Reel to Real: Making the Most of Movies with Youth.*

As I read the study guide, I want to go back into the Harry Potter books and into the Bible to consider matters I had not thought about before, to be led to passages of Scripture I had not previously associated with certain elements of the Harry Potter books, to think further about parallels I had not seen for myself or fully considered. I am looking forward to doing so with a group of peers (which will create a different experience than the one we had in a group of children, teens, and adults together). I am sure that when I do, and when you do, we will find even more to engage our imaginations, enrich our spiritual lives, and connect us to others in the group as we share that literary and spiritual interchange of ideas.

In speaking on these topics, I have coined the slogan: Be a reader! Be a thinker! Be a seeker! In life as in Quidditch, it seems to be that it is nearly always the seekers who win the game. I pray that you and each member of your group will fully enjoy the Harry Potter stories and all the discussion they generate. I am grateful to Skip Parvin for helping you do that well.

One final point needs to be addressed. You will probably run across some Christians who are opposed to the Harry Potter stories on biblical grounds. I recommend that you do not argue with them or try to convince them that they need to see these books as you do for several reasons. Chances are good that such an argument would be futile. Those in opposing camps on Harry Potter tend to look at literature in two different ways, to define the terms differently, and to reference different sources. Therefore, the arguments are not usually productive and often are destructive, leading to enmity, strife, division, dissentions, and factions. These are condemned along with sorcery in Galatians 5.

Christians who share many core beliefs, including opposition to witchcraft because the Bible forbids it, have come to hold strong convictions both for and against Harry Potter. Some are strongly in favor of the books, seeing them primarily as classic children's literature. Some are strongly opposed, seeing them primarily as being *about* witchcraft or at least too close for comfort because youngsters may be led into real witchcraft; or they think the stories imply that those who enjoy them either do not take the real dangers of the occult seriously or do not mind celebrating that which God has forbidden. Therefore, these issues are briefly considered up front in this study guide. I saw this to be such an important prerequisite (in response to the Bible's admonitions in Romans 14) that I felt compelled to write another book *before* I could write *The Gospel according to Harry Potter* with a clear conscience. If you are as yet uncertain about your convictions regarding this controversy, or if you are dealing with someone who strongly objects to the books (or your enjoyment of them), I suggest you read that book first. In *What's a Christian to Do with Harry Potter?* my aim was to help readers come to their own convictions with settled confidence. You can also give it to those who object to your enjoyment of the Harry Potter stories so that you personally do not have to argue. Since the controversy arises repeatedly, I have also created a section on my web site where you can find articles and resources related to Harry Potter from a Christian perspective. Those can be found at www.ConnieNeal.com.

Arguments aside, I am pleased to introduce you to Skip Parvin and the excellent resource he has written to help you and your group go further in your enjoyment of Harry Potter and the spiritual themes that the stories can awaken for you to think about and discuss.

CONNIE NEAL
April 2003

Introduction

Adapt yourselves no longer to the pattern of this present world, but let your minds be remade and your whole nature thus transformed. Then you will be able to discern the will of God, and to know what is good, acceptable and perfect.

Rom. 12:2 NEB

Unless you have been sojourning in isolation on some Himalayan mountaintop, you probably realize that a rip-roaring controversy is raging throughout Christendom in regard to our young friend Harry Potter. Just type "Harry Potter + Christian" into your favorite Internet search engine and watch the hits start rolling (I got about 275,000 search results the last time I did this). Should or shouldn't Christians be reading the Harry Potter books and watching the movies? What exactly are J. K. Rowling's motives and intentions? Christians have struggled with these and other questions since the first Harry Potter book was published in 1998.

The fact that I have written this study guide demonstrates where I stand on the issue. Connie Neal, the author on whose work this study guide is founded, has done a most excellent job of demonstrating what Harry Potter has to offer Christians. I still feel, however, that some apologetics are in order. If you are considering using this study guide, then you should know my perspective on all this.

I find all of the attempts to set up some complex criteria as to what constitutes "good" and "safe" fantasy literature and what constitutes "dangerous" or "subversive" fantasy literature intriguing. Complex webs of reasoning are being spun to justify J. R. R. Tolkien and C. S. Lewis as "appropriate" fantasy writers and to disparage J. K. Rowling as an "inappropriate" fantasy writer (at least with regard to Christian readers and moviegoers). While I find this a healthy, productive, and necessary theological discussion, I think it is a waste of time when it comes to the Harry Potter phenomenon. Some market researchers have estimated that two-thirds of American children ages six to seventeen years old have read one or more of the books, and 79 percent of those who have read Harry Potter books have seen the first movie. As my grandmother used to say, "No sense fixing the barn door after the horse is long gone." Obviously we cannot prevent children (and adults, for that matter) from being exposed to Harry Potter. So as Christians, what do we do? We use Harry Potter to teach Christian theology, ethics, and values. We teach people to think theologically and help them to become discerning Christian analysts when it comes to popular culture.

In Romans 12:2, Paul does not suggest that we take a monastic point of view and isolate ourselves from the world, because he knows that it is not possible to convert the world to Jesus Christ without actually living in it and associating with people who are inherently secular in their beliefs and outlook. Paul instead stresses discernment, one of the key gifts of the Holy Spirit. Paul says we should no longer "adapt" ourselves to the "pattern of this present world." If we follow his spiritual advice, then we are transformed and we will be able to discern what is "good, acceptable and perfect." The Holy Spirit becomes our guide in this discerning process. I would think that the difference between fantasy and reality would be right at the top of the Holy Spirit's list of what Christians need to be able to discern.

My theology is creation centered. This means that I find the foundation for theological reflection about God in my creativity and the creativity of others. Therefore, I do not run from the world, but embrace it in the hope that every day I might understand it a little bit better than the day before. If we ignore what the world is thinking, how can we keep the gospel relevant and frame it in a way that it will be heard and understood?

Throughout the history of Christianity, some segment of the Christian community has been at war with popular culture. Attempts are constantly being made to "shield" Christians from unhealthy influences that would "corrupt" them with worldliness. My impression is that it is impossible to avoid living in the world without physically leaving it. As one of the oldest Christian clichés states, "We must be in the world but not of the world." All human beings are given spiritual intuition to discern the prevenient grace that God has sprinkled liberally throughout the intricate interweavings of the world in which we live. This means we often find evidence of grace in the most unlikely places. If people have stopped looking to the institutional church for grace, then perhaps we should begin to help them see the grace that abounds in the world around them.

Ultimately, I think attempts by Christians to try to control what people do or do not read or do or do not watch are inevitably futile. For me, the bottom line has to do with what people *are* reading and watching. If we begin with what people know, we can help them to discover what they need to know. To disdain popular culture as a source of theological reflection is to limit the ways in which the gospel is communicated. I believe Harry Potter is a valuable starting point for evangelism and Christian education. Let's use this incredible phenomenon to offer the world Jesus Christ.

SKIP PARVIN

How to Use This Guide

In creating this study guide, we felt that it would be easier in group experiences to use the first two Harry Potter films and Connie Neal's book *The Gospel according to Harry Potter* as the foundation for these sessions. Obviously, many in your group will have read the books as well. This will only enhance the quality of discussion. Each of the sessions is designed to stand alone, and we have provided enough in the way of activities and discussion questions for each session to fill at least an hour. You will either need to view the film your group is discussing first, or show excerpts from the films to facilitate the discussion.

Both *Harry Potter and the Sorcerer's Stone* and *Harry Potter and the Chamber of Secrets* are available on DVD and VHS. The former will require two hours and thirty-two minutes to view in its entirety; the latter, two hours and forty-one minutes. An appendix is provided with scene indices that will allow you to quickly locate various excerpts that you might wish to show to your group before or during discussion.

While each session has been created with youth and young adults in mind, we feel that the sessions can be converted easily to work well with adults. The setting for using these sessions is left up to the leader, and there are several options. The leader can use them as a youth group program, a Sunday school class, a Bible study, or in any other educational setting. The sessions can be used wherever a television and a VCR and/or DVD player are available.

Despite the fact that each chapter is designed to stand alone, several of the sessions can be used in combination to form a Harry Potter retreat or lock-in. Retreats or lock-ins can be structured to focus on either or both of the Harry Potter films.

Always preview the film or scenes you will be using in your discussion. Don't ever assume that you can remember everything about a film or scene. You will be surprised at how much you can forget.

This guide is created to accompany the book *The Gospel according to Harry Potter* by Connie Neal, published by Westminster John Knox Press. Though it is not necessary, it will be helpful if each participant has a copy of that book. You as a leader will certainly want to have a copy. The book can be found in your local bookstore, on the web at www.wjkbooks.com, or by calling 1-800-227-2872. If you call, you may wish to inquire about quantity discounts. Connie's first book about the Harry Potter phenomenon, *What's a Christian to Do with Harry Potter?* from Waterbrook Press, would also be valuable to any leader as a supplemental resource.

The two movies, released by Warner Home Video, are available at your local video store, bookstore, or online at Amazon.com. The books *Harry Potter and the Sorcerer's Stone* and *Harry Potter and the Chamber of Secrets*, both by J. K. Rowling, were published in North America by Scholastic Press and in the United Kingdom by Bloomsbury Children's Books, and are available wherever books are sold.

One

What Should a Christian Think about Magic, Wizardry, and Sorcery?

Supplementary Reading: Introduction (pp. vii–xiii), Notes to the Reader (pp. xiv–xvi), Introduction to Book One (pp. 3–5) and The Mystery of the Shrinking Door Keys (pp. 60–62) in *The Gospel according to Harry Potter.*

Useful Scenes from the Films: Scene 8 (The Boy Who Lived), Scene 30 (Man with Two Faces), Scene 31 (Magic Touch), and Scene 32 (Mark of Love) in *Harry Potter and the Sorcerer's Stone.* Scene 2 (Dobby's Warning), Scene 4 (The Burrow), Scene 17 (Dueling Club), Scene 21 (Harry and Ron Transformed), and Scene 35 (Dobby's Reward) in *Harry Potter and the Chamber of Secrets.*

Note to Leader: This introductory session is longer than the others and can actually be divided into three sessions if necessary. The first session would deal with the section on the relationship between reality and fantasy; the second would deal with the Old Testament text; and the third would deal with the New Testament text.

Old Testament Scripture Lesson (1 Kings 18:20–24): So Ahab sent to all the Israelites, and assembled the prophets at Mount Carmel. Elijah then came near to all the people, and said, "How long will you go limping with two different opinions? If the LORD is God, follow him; but if Baal, then follow him." The

3

people did not answer him a word. Then Elijah said to the people, "I, even I only, am left a prophet of the LORD; but Baal's prophets number four hundred fifty. Let two bulls be given to us; let them choose one bull for themselves, cut it in pieces, and lay it on the wood, but put no fire to it; I will prepare the other bull and lay it on the wood, but put no fire to it. Then you call on the name of your god and I will call on the name of the LORD; the god who answers by fire is indeed God." All the people answered, "Well spoken!"

New Testament Scripture Lesson (Acts 8:9–24): Now a certain man named Simon had previously practiced magic in the city and amazed the people of Samaria, saying that he was someone great. All of them, from the least to the greatest, listened to him eagerly, saying, "This man is the power of God that is called Great." And they listened eagerly to him because for a long time he had amazed them with his magic. But when they believed Philip, who was proclaiming the good news about the kingdom of God and the name of Jesus Christ, they were baptized, both men and women. Even Simon himself believed. After being baptized, he stayed constantly with Philip and was amazed when he saw the signs and great miracles that took place.

Now when the apostles at Jerusalem heard that Samaria had accepted the word of God, they sent Peter and John to them. The two went down and prayed for them that they might receive the Holy Spirit (for as yet the Spirit had not come upon any of them; they had only been baptized in the name of the Lord Jesus). Then Peter and John laid their hands on them, and they received the Holy Spirit. Now when Simon saw that the Spirit was given through the laying on of the apostles' hands, he offered them money, saying, "Give me also this power so that anyone on whom I lay my hands may receive the Holy Spirit." But Peter said to him, "May your silver perish with you, because you thought you could obtain God's gift with money! You have no part or share in this, for your heart is not right before God. Repent therefore of this wickedness of yours, and pray to the Lord that, if possible, the intent of your heart may be forgiven you. For I see that you are in the gall of bitterness and the chains of wickedness." Simon answered, "Pray for me to the Lord, that nothing of what you have said may happen to me."

Other Scripture Texts That Refer to Magic, Sorcery, Wizardry, and Witchcraft

- Exodus 22:18 (Female sorcerers are to be sentenced to death.)
- Leviticus 19:26 (The people of Israel are commanded not to practice augury or witchcraft.)
- Leviticus 19:31 and 20:6 (The people of Israel are warned not to consult wizards or mediums.)
- Leviticus 20:27 (Men and women who are wizards or mediums are sentenced to death.)
- Deuteronomy 18:10–12 (The people of Israel are warned against the practices associated with sorcery.)
- 1 Samuel 28:3–20 (After the death of Samuel, Saul expels the wizards and mediums from Israel, but later goes out in disguise in order to have a medium help him make contact with Samuel.)
- 2 Kings 21:1–6 and 2 Chronicles 33:1–9 (Manasseh is admonished for consorting with mediums and wizards among his other evil deeds.)
- Nahum 2:8–3:7 (Nineveh is compared to an alluring sorceress.)
- Acts 19:18–20 (Believers who had practiced magic gather and destroy their books.)
- Galatians 5:19–21 (Sorcery is listed as a work of the flesh.)
- Revelation 18:23 (Babylon is admonished for deceiving the nations with her sorcery.)

Activity: Have the definitions below written out on a marker board or newsprint, but cover them so the group will not be able to see or read them yet. Ask the group to describe the difference between fantasy and reality: What does fantasy mean? Record their suggestions and comments. Have the group work together to create its own definition of *fantasy*. Do the same for *reality, magic,* and *wizard*. After they are finished, reveal the dictionary definitions and discuss them. How are your group's definitions similar to the dictionary definitions? How do they differ?

Some Definitions

Fantasy Conceived through imagination or vivid visionary fancy.

Reality (real) That which truly exists or happens in fact; not the product of imagination.

Magic The pretended practice of creating effects or seeming to control persons or events by charms, spells, and rituals, which call on supposed natural or supernatural forces. Magic is often associated with sorcery and witchcraft in fantasy literature.

Wizard A powerful magician or sorcerer. The original meaning of *wizard* is simply "a wise man or sage."

Questions for Discussion

- Do you think that the Harry Potter books and movies are an elaborate fantasy, or do you think that there are elements of these books and movies about which Christians should be concerned? (Opinions will probably vary. Some may argue that Harry Potter is presented as a harmless fantasy. Others may see aspects of Harry's relationships and exploits that concern them. Allow the members of the group to express their opinions openly without devaluing other viewpoints.)

- What are some of the aspects of the Harry Potter books and movies that should concern us from a Christian point of view?

(Obvious answers will include wizardry, witchcraft, spell casting, potions, and other ideas associated with Harry's magical world. Some may express concern about Harry's association with strange and otherworldly beings (such as Dobby and Moaning Myrtle). Others may cite the possible connection between magic and occult practices. Be sure to deal with all of the ideas presented objectively, and allow members of the group to disagree with one another as they discuss.)

- Can a Christian read a book or watch a movie that contains imaginary elements of fantasy based in magic without taking the idea of wizardry, witchcraft, or sorcery seriously? (Again, opinions will vary. Be sure to be open to all viewpoints.)

- Can you name any other books, movies, or television shows that use the idea of an imaginary world in which magic exists to tell a story? (The most immediate response will probably be Tolkien's *Lord of the Rings* trilogy, as the movies have been released concurrent with the Harry Potter movies. Others will likely suggest *Chronicles of Narnia* by C. S. Lewis. A wide variety of popular television shows may also be suggested as well, such as *Buffy the Vampire Slayer, Charmed, Sabrina the Teenaged Witch, Yu-Gi-Oh, Dragon Ball Z,* and *Pokemon,* to name a few. Another excellent example to discuss would be the famous Mickey Mouse short, *The Sorcerer's Apprentice.*)

- Have a member of the group read Romans 12:2. What does Paul have to say about our relationship to the world? (Paul reminds us not to "conform" or "adapt" to the present world but to be transformed by our relationship with Jesus Christ through the Holy Spirit. The Holy Spirit then guides us in discerning what is "good and acceptable and perfect.")

- Do you think that Paul's spiritual advice about discernment is a good foundation for dealing with what we find in Harry Potter?

- Do you believe that the Holy Spirit helps us to discern the difference between fantasy and reality?

- What about others who have not accepted Jesus Christ and do not have the Holy Spirit in their lives? How do they discern this difference? (Obviously, spiritual discernment is a problem for a person who is not consciously spiritual. We as Christians often need to help others to discern the movement of God's Spirit in the world. We can then use Harry Potter to begin a spiritual discussion and witness to the power of the Holy Spirit in our lives.)

Activity: Assign a different person in the group one of the texts listed under "Other Scripture Texts That Refer to Magic, Sorcery, Wizardry, and Witchcraft." Have them read and share their scriptures with one another.

- Why do you think the Old Testament law was so harsh in dealing with magic and sorcery? (The practices were associated with other religions that threatened to corrupt the Israelites in their worship of the one true God, Yahweh. The law was intended to stress the importance of leaving these practices behind, even to the point of suggesting that practitioners be put to death. However, it needs to be noted that there are a multitude of offenses under the Levitical Code for which the death penalty was suggested.)

- Do you think the magic and sorcery in the fantasy world of Harry Potter are the same as the magic and sorcery prohibited by Old Testament law? (Opinions will vary. The key difference here is that this Old Testament prohibition was focused on people who were actually attempting to use magic and sorcery in the real world to produce real, often evil, results. Attempting to use magic to manipulate the real world would undermine and challenge the power of Yahweh.)

Activity: Have a member (or members) of the group read the story of the confrontation between Elijah and the priests of Baal, which is excerpted on pages 3–4. (The complete story can be found in 1 Kings 18:17–40 if you would like to have your group read it all. If you would not, then it would probably be a good idea to read aloud the excerpt and paraphrase the rest.

- What do you think Elijah is doing here? (Here Elijah seeks to demonstrate the power of Yahweh by setting up a competition. He challenges the priests of Baal to call on their god to bring fire down upon a sacrificial offering, and he will ask the same of Yahweh.)

- Why do you think Elijah did this? (More than likely, the priests of Baal used what we might call "magic tricks," in the way that, for instance, the famous stage magician David Copperfield might use magic, that is, to convince people that they had power over the natural world. Elijah's intent is to expose Baal's priests as powerless frauds.)

- What is the outcome of the competition? (Elijah demonstrates through the competition that real power comes only from the one true God, Yahweh, not through tricks and illusion.)

- What is this story about? (The fundamental idea here is that God and God alone has power over the natural world, which God has created.)

Activity: Have a member (or members) of the group read the story of Simon the magician from Acts 8:9–24.

- What is this story about? (Simon is a former magician who mistakes the power of the Holy Spirit for magical power and offers to "buy" the power from Peter and John. What Simon is really after is the power to "give" the Spirit through the laying on of hands.)

- What does the story tell us about Simon's magical powers? (He was so good at magic that people were amazed and listened to what he had to say, giving him great authority.)

- Did the people who witnessed Simon's magic believe that it was a sign of God's power being manifested through Simon? (Yes. In fact, the people actually say, "This man is the power of God that is called Great.")

- What changes their minds? (Philip tells them the gospel story, and they give their lives to Jesus Christ. Even Simon accepts Jesus and is baptized. Simon is amazed at the signs and miracles that take place in Jesus' name. When the people see the real power of God's Spirit, then magic and illusion pale in comparison.)

- Why do you think Simon wanted to buy from Peter and John the ability to give the gift of the Holy Spirit through the laying on of hands? (Simon had once had great authority among the people, which he had gained through his ability to astound them with his magic. When he saw the power of the Holy Spirit come upon people, he wanted to be the one to control the giving of that power.)

- What is Simon's key error in judgment? (He mistakes the power of the Holy Spirit for something that can be learned or bought. Even as today magicians will sell one another the secrets to the illusions behind their tricks, Simon had most probably obtained some of his magic tricks by purchasing them from other magicians. Simon did not realize that the Holy Spirit was an extension of God's love through the unmerited and unearned gift of grace.)

- What does this story have to teach us about the relationship between magic and the true power of God?

Prayer: O God our Creator, source of all true spiritual power, help us to always be able to tell the difference between fantasy and reality. Keep us mindful of the fact that the illusion of worldly power cannot begin to compare with the power of your Holy Spirit in our lives. Help us to be transformed by that Spirit so that we will always be able to discern what is "good and acceptable and perfect" in your love. Amen.

Something to Talk About: A good way to supplement this session would be to bring an actual magician in to perform for your group (you may even have one in your congregation). Make sure that the magician is willing to answer questions about magic and the art of illusion. Perhaps he or she will even be willing to teach the group a simple trick or two to give them a behind-the-scenes look at how magic tricks work.

Two

The Love of Power
versus the Power of Love

Supplementary Reading: The Quest for the Sorcerer's Stone (pp. 33–35) and Why the Evil One Could Not Touch Harry (p. 48) in *The Gospel according to Harry Potter.*

Useful Scenes from the Films: Scene 8 (The Boy Who Lived), Scene 31 (Magic Touch), and Scene 32 (Mark of Love) in *Harry Potter and the Sorcerer's Stone.* Scene 24 (Petrified), Scene 33 (Healing Powers), and Scene 34 (Out of the Hat) in *Harry Potter and the Chamber of Secrets.*

Old Testament Scripture Lessons (1 Chronicles 29:10–13): Then David blessed the LORD in the presence of all the assembly; David said: "Blessed are you, O LORD, the God of our ancestor Israel, forever and ever. Yours, O LORD, are the greatness, the power, the glory, the victory, and the majesty; for all that is in the heavens and on the earth is yours; yours is the kingdom, O LORD, and you are exalted as head above all. Riches and honor come from you, and you rule over all. In your hand are power and might; and it is in your hand to make great and to give strength to all. And now, our God, we give thanks to you and praise your glorious name.

(Zechariah 4:6b): Not by might, nor by power, but by my spirit, says the LORD of hosts.

"A foolish young man I was then, full of ridiculous ideas about good and evil. Lord Voldemort showed me how wrong I was. There is no good and evil, there is only power, and those too weak to seek it."

—Professor Quirrell, explaining to Harry why he chose to serve Lord Voldemort

"Your mother died to save you. If there is one thing Voldemort cannot understand, it is love. He didn't realize that love as powerful as your mother's for you leaves its own mark. Not a scar, no visible sign . . . to have been loved so deeply, even though the person who loved us is gone, will give us some protection forever. It is in your very skin. Quirrell, full of hatred, greed, and ambition, sharing his soul with Voldemort, could not touch you for this reason. It was agony to touch a person marked by something so good."

—Albus Dumbledore, explaining to Harry why Professor Quirrell could not harm him

Excerpts from *Harry Potter and the Sorcerer's Stone,* by J. K. Rowling (New York: Scholastic Press, 1998).

New Testament Scripture Lesson (2 Peter 1:3–7): His divine power has given us everything needed for life and godliness, through the knowledge of him who called us by his own glory and goodness. Thus he has given us, through these things, his precious and very great promises, so that through them you may escape from the corruption that is in the world because of lust, and may become participants of the divine nature. For this very reason, you must make every effort to support your faith with goodness, and goodness with knowledge, and knowledge with self-control, and self-control with endurance, and endurance with godliness, and godliness with mutual affection, and mutual affection with love.

Activity: On a marker board or newsprint, draw a chart that looks like the one below, with the exception that the chart should be blank except for the top row. Ask the members of the group to list the characters they believe have power, and then fill in the answers to the questions as they discuss. (Obviously your group can include characters not listed here). The answers below are only suggested guidelines for possible answers. Your group may come up with different answers or suggestions.

Character	Degree of Power	Type	Weakness	Use of Power?
Harry	Great power	Harry will one day be a great wizard, but as of now his power is immature.	Harry's primary weakness is his compassion. He will always give himself up for others.	He fights evil and injustice in whatever forms they present themselves.
Dumbledore	Great power	He is the greatest living wizard.	He will only use his power for good and will never call on the dark arts.	He acts as a force for good behind the scenes.
Voldemort	Great power	He is the most powerful evil wizard to ever live.	He can always be defeated in the end by love and goodness. He currently has no physical body.	He seeks total domination and immortality and will do anything to achieve his purposes.

Character	Degree of Power	Type	Weakness	Use of Power?
Hagrid	Significant power	He is a caretaker who uses his power to guide and protect Harry.	He sometimes bumbles around, is easily tempted, and cannot keep a secret.	He acts as a force for good in the best ways he can.
Ron	Developing power	In addition to his wizardry skills, Ron is courageous, strong, and loyal.	His magic is always backfiring on him.	He acts as part of Harry's "team" to work for good.
Hermione	Developing power	In addition to her wizardry skills, Hermione has great intellect and is incredibly resourceful. She is the best at incantations.	While she often appears supremely self-confident, she is actually deeply sensitive and easily hurt.	She acts as part of Harry's "team" to work for good.
Gilderoy Lockhart	Limited power	He claims great power but this is mostly lies.	He is a coward and a fraud.	In the end he works to oppose Harry.

Questions for Discussion

- Why do people seek power? (Answers will vary. Some seek power in order to control the world around them or to control others. Some want to use power to gain material possessions and impress others. Others believe that having power will give them an opportunity to change the world. Still others need power to bolster their own low self-esteem.)

- Read the quote in which Quirrell explains to Harry why he chose to follow Lord Voldemort. Why do Quirrell and Voldemort seek power? (Voldemort seeks to have everyone else in the world be subject to his will. He also wants to become immortal. He is willing to do anything in order to have that kind of worldly power.)

- Does Harry have power? What is the difference between Harry and Voldemort? (Harry has power, but, as of yet, he does not understand the reason he was given so great a gift. Unlike Voldemort, Harry realizes that "with great power comes great responsibility," to quote another movie hero—Spider-Man.)

- Read the quote in which Dumbledore explains to Harry why Professor Quirrell could not harm him. What, according to Dumbledore, is the greatest power of all? (Love. The one thing that those who are absolutely selfish and evil cannot understand is the power of love. To reinforce this idea you could have a member of the group read 1 Corinthians 13.)

- Have a member of the group read 1 Chronicles 29:10–13. What does King David have to say about power? (David is revered as the greatest leader that Israel ever had. Here David acknowledges before all of Israel that the only true power in creation comes from God. He gives thanks to God for his worldly power and the benefits it has brought him and the nation of Israel.)

- What is the difference between the way Voldemort looks at power and the way David looks at power? (Voldemort mistakenly believes that worldly power is ultimate power. Voldemort is so self-centered that he cannot conceive of a power greater than himself. David, on the other hand, understands that all real power comes from God. Even though David often abused the power God gave him and failed many times in his life, he always understood that God was ultimately in control. A good example of this is Psalm 51. David wrote this psalm after the great sin he committed in order to marry Bathsheba. In it he acknowledges God's absolute power over him and realizes that he is nothing without a right relationship with God.)

- Have a member of the group read the short verse from the prophet Zechariah. What does this have to say about the true nature of power? (Nothing that matters eternally is created by exercising power and might in the world. The power of this world fades. It is only through God's Spirit that the true purposes of God's eternal power are realized.)

- Have a member of the group read 2 Peter 1:3–7. What does the writer of 2 Peter have to say about true power? (First, the writer of 2 Peter is convinced that the only important power is "divine power." He is not talking about worldly power, but power that comes through God's Spirit. If we base our life on God's divine power, then we are able to escape the corruption of this world and have a relationship with God's divine nature.)

- What does the writer of 2 Peter feel is the highest expression of power in our lives? (Love)

- How do we obtain this power? (It is a process of spiritual maturation. Faith leads to goodness, goodness leads to knowledge, knowledge leads to self-control, self-control leads to endurance, endurance leads to godliness, godliness leads to mutual affection, and mutual affection leads to love. Note that "mutual affection" and love are not the same to the writer of 2 Peter. For him, mutual affection is the reflection of God's love that we see in each other and that leads us to the true power found in God's love.)

- Does Harry exhibit the kind of power that the writer of 2 Peter is talking about? (The simple answer would be yes. Harry always places his love for others above his own needs and safety. Harry is working through the steps to spiritual maturity that are outlined by the writer of 2 Peter. *It is also important to note that Harry's most significant accomplishments have nothing to do with using magic.* They have to do with courage and self-sacrifice. In Harry's best moments, he exhibits all the qualities expressed in the passage from 2 Peter.)

Prayer: O Lord our God, please help us to remember that the only real power we can ever experience in this life is the power of your love. Show us how to make your Spirit the foundation for all we do. Help us to overcome our own selfish desires and concentrate on your will and the needs of others. Help us to change the world by changing ourselves. Amen.

Something to Talk About: Have the members of your group talk to their parents and/or friends in the coming week about how they understand power. Who has power in our world? What makes us feel powerless? Can some people use their power to change the world? What are some good examples? How is power abused? What are some examples of the abuse of power? What is the evidence that love is the greatest power in our lives?

Three

Many Gifts, One Body

Supplementary Reading: The Leaky Cauldron: A Door to an Unseen World (pp. 15–16), The Sorting (pp. 22–24), and This Isn't Magic, It's Logic! (pp. 39–40) in *The Gospel according to Harry Potter.*

Useful Scenes from the Films: Scene 2 (Vanishing Glass), Scene 4 (Keeper of the Keys), Scene 7 (Ollivander's), and Scene 12 (Sorting Hat) in *Harry Potter and the Sorcerer's Stone.* Scene 17 (Dueling Club) and Scene 34 (Out of the Hat) in *Harry Potter and the Chamber of Secrets.*

Old Testament Scripture Lesson (Isaiah 49:1–3): Listen to me, O coastlands, pay attention, you peoples from far away! The LORD called me before I was born, while I was in my mother's womb he named me. He made my mouth like a sharp sword, in the shadow of his hand he hid me; he made me a polished arrow, in his quiver he hid me away. And he said to me, "You are my servant, Israel, in whom I will be glorified."

New Testament Scripture Lesson (1 Corinthians 12:4–7): Now there are varieties of gifts, but the same Spirit; and there are varieties of services, but the same Lord; and there are varieties of activities, but it is the same God who activates all of them in everyone. To each is given the manifestation of the Spirit for the common good.

Questions for Discussion

- Have a member of your group read the passage from Isaiah. What does Isaiah have to say about the relationship between his gifts and his calling to become a prophet? (Isaiah says that the gifts that would make him a great prophet of God were present from the time he was conceived. He says God gave him a "mouth like a sharp sword" and made him like a "polished arrow." The gifts and the calling both contribute to one another.)

- Obviously, Harry has been called to fight the evil that Voldemort represents. What are his gifts? (Answers could include but not be limited to: He is a powerful wizard. He can resist the temptation to use his power for evil purposes. He can hear and speak Parseltongue. He has a natural sense of spiritual intuition. He is an exceptional leader. He has great compassion.)

- Do you think Harry's gifts are related to his calling? (As the story progresses, we see that Harry seems to feel that his calling to fight the evil represented in Lord Voldemort is unavoidable. All of his gifts point him in that direction.)

- Isaiah feels that he was predestined to become God's prophet. Do you think Harry was predestined to take the role he assumes in fighting evil? (Answers will depend on how members of your group view the idea of a predetermined destiny. It seems that J. K. Rowling has gone to great lengths to demonstrate that Harry has a special purpose in the world. It is the sum total of his gifts that point him in that direction.)

- Do you think that Harry could deny his gifts? (The nature of a gift is that it must be accepted. Harry definitely has free will. Even though he does not choose to deny his gifts, we have to believe that he could.)

- Does Harry possess all the gifts necessary to defeat the evil that is present in Voldemort? (Harry has the power necessary to battle Voldemort one on one. However, it is the combination of the gifts of those close to him that put him in the position to fight and defeat Voldemort. Dumbledore, Hagrid, Hermione, Ron, and many others contribute to bringing about the defeat of Voldemort.)

- Have a member of the group read 1 Corinthians 12:7–27. Does this image of the body of Christ remind you of the way the gifts of Harry and his friends work together to defeat evil? (While the gifts of Harry and his friends cannot literally be considered gifts of the Spirit, their gifts do work together for the "common good" just as Paul describes.)

- Based on Paul's idea of the body of Christ, how do you see Harry and his friends as "many members, yet one body"? (Harry could not have done what he did alone. Each of the persons closest to Harry contributes significantly to the defeat of Voldemort. Dumbledore provides mentoring, wisdom, and protection. Hagrid has a gift for support and consultation. Ron has courage, loyalty, and strength. Hermione has a keen intellect and an analytical mind. The combination of the gifts working together is more powerful than any one gift expressed alone.)

- How does Harry discover his gifts? (Harry comes to the gradual realization that he has certain gifts. For instance, at the zoo Harry finds that he is able to speak to the snake, and he inadvertently makes the glass disappear, causing Dudley to fall in the water. As Harry discovers his gifts he begins to accept them, and they become a part of his maturation process.)

- Do you feel that you have spiritual gifts? How did you discover them?

- Has the process through which you discovered your gifts been similar to Harry's discovery of his?

- Do the gifts of other people in your group work together in the same way that the gifts of Harry's group work together? Do you see evidence in your group that supports Paul's idea of the body of Christ?

Prayer: O God our Creator, we know that each of us has been given gifts in your Spirit. Help us to discern those gifts and use them in the way that you intend. Help us to see the spiritual gifts in the people around us and understand the ways in which those gifts can work together in the body of Christ. Amen.

Something to Talk About: Have the members of your group discuss the idea of spiritual gifts with family, friends, and other persons they respect by asking them these questions: Do you see yourself as having spiritual gifts? What spiritual gifts do you believe you have? How did you discover your spiritual gifts? How do you see your spiritual gifts contributing to the body of Christ?

Four

What Does It Mean to Be Called?

Supplementary Reading: The Curse of Death and the Boy Who Lived (pp. 6–7), A Lightning Bolt Scar (pp. 8–9), Scars Can Come in Handy (pp. 10–11), The Unstoppable Invitation (pp. 12–14), The Sorting (pp. 22–24), and A Songbird and an Old Hat (pp. 76–79) in *The Gospel according to Harry Potter*.

Useful Scenes from the Films: Scene 1 (Doorstep Delivery), Scene 3 (Letters from No One), Scene 4 (Keeper of the Keys), and Scene 12 (Sorting Hat) in *Harry Potter and the Sorcerer's Stone*.

Old Testament Scripture Lesson (1 Samuel 3:4–10): Then the LORD called, "Samuel! Samuel!" and he said, "Here I am!" and ran to Eli, and said, "Here I am, for you called me." But he said, "I did not call; lie down again." So he went and lay down. The LORD called again, "Samuel!" Samuel got up and went to Eli, and said, "Here I am, for you called me." But he said, "I did not call, my son; lie down again." Now Samuel did not yet know the LORD, and the word of the LORD had not yet been revealed to him. The LORD called Samuel again, a third time. And he got up and went to Eli, and said, "Here I am, for you called me." Then Eli perceived that the LORD was calling the boy. Therefore Eli said to Samuel, "Go, lie down; and if he calls you, you shall say, 'Speak, LORD, for your servant is listening.'" So Samuel went and lay down in his place.

Hagrid: You're a wizard, Harry!

Harry: I'm a what?

"So I *should* be in Slytherin," Harry said, looking desperately into Dumbledore's face. "The Sorting Hat could see Slytherin's power in me, and it—"

"Put you in Gryffindor," said Dumbledore calmly. "Listen to me, Harry. You happen to have many qualities Salazar Slytherin prized in his hand-picked students. His own very rare gift, Parseltongue—resourcefulness—determination—a certain disregard for rules," he added, his mustache quivering again. "Yet the Sorting Hat placed you in Gryffindor. You know why that was. Think."

"It only put me in Gryffindor," said Harry in a defeated voice, "because I asked not to go in Slytherin. . . ."

"*Exactly,*" said Dumbledore, beaming once more. "Which makes you *very different* from Tom Riddle. It is our choices, Harry, that show what we truly are, far more than our abilities."

Excerpted from *Harry Potter and the Chamber of Secrets* by J. K. Rowling (New York: Scholastic Press, 1999)

Now the LORD came and stood there, calling as before, "Samuel! Samuel!" And Samuel said, "Speak, for your servant is listening."

New Testament Scripture Lesson (Ephesians 4:1–6): I therefore, the prisoner in the Lord, beg you to lead a life worthy of the calling to which you have been called, with all humility and gentleness, with patience, bearing with one another in love, making every effort to maintain the unity of the Spirit in the bond of peace. There is one body and one Spirit, just as you were called to the one hope of your calling, one Lord, one faith, one baptism, one God and Father of all, who is above all and through all and in all.

Calling throughout the Bible

The Calling of Abraham: Genesis 12:1–4

The Calling of Moses: Exodus 3:2–4:20

The Calling of Samuel: 1 Samuel 3:1–20

The Calling of Isaiah: Isaiah 6:1–8

The Calling of Peter, Andrew, James, and John: Luke 5:1–11

The Calling of Saul (Paul): Acts 9:1–20

Activity: Divide the group into six smaller discussion groups and assign each of the smaller groups one of the examples of calling listed under "Calling throughout the Bible." Ask them to read the story assigned to them and to analyze it. Who is being called? Why is he being called? How is he called? Does it seem like he was prepared for the moment in which he is called? What are the expectations placed on the person being called? How does he respond?

When they are finished answering these questions, have the group gather back together to discuss what each small group discovered. On a marker board or newsprint, list the common elements of the calling experience. Have the group come up with its own definition of calling. Write this definition on the marker board or newsprint so that it can be referred to later in the session.

Questions for Discussion

- Based on your discussion of the different examples of calling from the Bible, do you think Harry Potter has a calling? (While it is certainly not a "divine" calling like those the group looked at together, Harry's life journey does share elements with the examples of calling listed here.)

- What are some of the similarities between Harry's sense of calling and the examples you looked at as a group? (Answers might include but not be limited to: There is a sense of urgency in the call. The person being called understands that there is something greater than himself at work in the call. The call is, for all intents and purposes, irresistible. It is as if each person called was predestined to fill the role for which he is being called. The expectations and outcome of the call are not made completely clear at the time of the call itself.)

> ## Some Definitions
>
> **Calling** Being summoned by God for a specific purpose. An internal spiritual drive to follow a specific course of action in one's life. Sometimes referred to as a vocation.
>
> **Vocation** A desire to fulfill a specific purpose with one's life or to choose a certain career toward which one perceives himself or herself to be called.

- What has Harry been doing in his life that sets the stage for his calling? (Harry has spent most of his life wondering, "Who am I?" He seeks to understand why he is different from other people. In the end he realizes that it is what he must become that will show him who he really is. That is the essence of the calling experience.)

- What evidence is there that points to Harry's being called? (Some answers might include: He knows that he does not belong in the world in which he finds himself. He has a nagging feeling that he needs to be doing something far greater than his life presently allows. The letters that come to Harry to invite him to attend Hogwarts are essentially irresistible, and he does not hesitate to accept the invitation. Other people recognize the special qualities in him that will lead to the call. He begins to discover that he is different from the rest of the world.)

- Have a member of the group read the quote in which Dumbledore discusses with Harry the essence of his experience with the Sorting Hat. What does this conversation tell us about Harry's calling? (Dumbledore makes it clear that it is Harry's ability to resist the temptation of the power of evil and then to choose the power of good that makes his calling special. Harry is different from Tom Riddle because he sees his calling as something greater than himself. Riddle, on the other hand, is only interested in his selfish need to dominate through worldly power.)

- Have members of the group read the definitions of *calling* and *vocation*. How does Harry's life journey reflect these definitions? What is missing? (What is missing is the divine element, the fact that it is God who calls. While Harry is obviously being called to something far greater than himself that will give his life purpose and serve the greater good by contributing to the defeat of evil, the call is not from God.)

- Have a member of the group read Ephesians 4:1–6. (Another excellent New Testament passage to facilitate this discussion is 2 Timothy 1:6–10.) What does this text tell us about the Christian understanding of calling? (First and foremost, the call comes from God. Second, all Christians have a calling that comes through the Holy Spirit. Third, this calling is a humble surrender to God's love and requires the person called to be patient as it is realized in his or her life. Fourth, it requires great courage to surrender ourselves to the calling God holds for us. And finally, it is not our purpose, but God's purpose that is being realized through our calling.)

- Discuss the particular call that pastors receive to become the leaders of spiritual communities. In what sense is this kind of calling different? (All Christians are called; the Bible is clear on this point. The calling to be a pastor, to lead a family of faith and take responsibility for its members' spiritual well-being, is simply a much more specific, specialized form of calling. As Christians mature in their faith, they will find that God's call becomes less general and more focused. The call to be a pastor is one way that God focuses God's call in the lives of various individuals.)

- What is God calling you to do?

Prayer: Dear God, help us to hear you when you call. Give us the strength and courage to respond to your expectations for our lives. Show us how we can be part of something greater than ourselves by surrendering to your will as we live in your love. Help us to become part of your desire to redeem all of your creation. Amen.

Something to Talk About: Have the members of your group seek out people they respect in your family of faith (other than the pastor) and discuss the idea of calling with them (remind them that *every* Christian is called, not just the pastor) by asking these questions: How do you define calling? Do you feel as if you have been called? What form did your calling take? What have you done to follow through on your calling? How has your calling changed your life?

Five

How Should We Deal with Temptation?

Supplementary Reading: Dumbledore's Dire Warning (pp. 25–26), Hagrid's Temptation (pp. 27–29), Professor Quirrell's Defense Against the Dark Arts Lessons (pp. 41–42), and Gilderoy Lockhart Goes Down! (pp. 72–75) in *The Gospel according to Harry Potter*.

Useful Scenes from the Films: Scene 12 (Sorting Hat), Scene 23 (Mirror of Erised), and Scene 24 (Norbert) in *Harry Potter and the Sorcerer's Stone*.

Old Testament Scripture Lesson (Psalm 10:3–6): For the wicked boast of the desires of their heart, those greedy for gain curse and renounce the LORD. In the pride of their countenance the wicked say, "God will not seek it out"; all their thoughts are, "There is no God." Their ways prosper at all times; your judgments are on high, out of their sight; as for their foes, they scoff at them. They think in their heart, "We shall not be moved; throughout all generations we shall not meet adversity."

New Testament Scripture Lessons (Luke 4:1–13): Jesus, full of the Holy Spirit, returned from the Jordan and was led by the Spirit in the wilderness, where for forty days he was tempted by the devil. He ate nothing at all during those days, and when they were over, he was famished. The devil said to him, "If you are the

Erised stra ehru oyt ube cafru oyt on wohsi. ("I show not your face but your heart's desire.")

—Inscription carved on the Mirror of Erised (*desire*, spelled backwards)

"It shows us nothing more or less than the deepest, most desperate desire of our hearts. You, who have never known your family, see them standing around you. Ronald Weasley, who has always been overshadowed by his brothers, sees himself standing alone, the best of all of them. However, this mirror will give us neither knowledge or truth. Men have wasted away before it, entranced by what they have seen, or been driven mad, not knowing if what it shows is real or even possible."

—Dumbledore, describing the power of the Mirror of Erised to Harry

Excerpted from *Harry Potter and the Sorcerer's Stone,* by J. K. Rowling (New York: Scholastic Press, 1998)

Son of God, command this stone to become a loaf of bread." Jesus answered him, "It is written, 'One does not live by bread alone.'"

Then the devil led him up and showed him in an instant all the kingdoms of the world. And the devil said to him, "To you I will give their glory and all this authority; for it has been given over to me, and I give it to anyone I please. If you, then, will worship me, it will all be yours." Jesus answered him, "It is written, 'Worship the Lord your God, and serve only him.'" Then the devil took him to Jerusalem, and placed him on the pinnacle of the temple, saying to him, "If you are the Son of God, throw yourself down from here, for it is written, 'He will command his angels concerning you, to protect you,' and 'On their hands they will bear you up, so that you will not dash your foot against a stone.'" Jesus answered him, "It is said, 'Do not put the Lord your God to the test.'" When the devil had finished every test, he departed from him until an opportune time.

(James 1:12–16): Blessed is anyone who endures temptation. Such a one has stood the test and will receive the crown of life that the Lord has promised to those who love him. No one, when tempted, should say, "I am being tempted by God"; for God cannot be tempted by evil and he himself tempts no one. But one is tempted by one's own desire, being lured and enticed by it; then, when that desire has conceived, it gives birth to sin, and that sin, when it is fully grown, gives birth to death. Do not be deceived, my beloved.

Activity: On a marker board or newsprint, draw a chart that looks like the one below, with the exception that the chart should be blank except for the first column (which lists the characters) and top row ("Greatest Temptations" and "Methods of Overcoming"). Ask the members of your group to fill in the blanks in relation to that character's temptations. (Again, your group can include characters and temptations not listed here; the answers below are only suggested guidelines for possible responses. Your group may come up with different answers or suggestions.)

Character	Greatest Temptations	Methods of Overcoming
Harry	He is tempted to turn his power to evil, to risk everything for a chance to be with his mother and father again.	He overcomes these temptations through strength of character and sheer force of will, and through his dedication to the principle that good must prevail.
Dumbledore	Given his power, maturity, and stage of life, he is primarily tempted by "creature comforts" (sherbet lemon drops and warm socks).	He has discovered that the tempting "good things" in life are only good as long as they are experienced in moderation. The things that make us the happiest are often quite simple.

Character	Greatest Temptations	Methods of Overcoming
Voldemort	He has given in to his temptation to achieve absolute power and seek immortality.	He yields to his temptation and destroys himself and others in the process.
Hagrid	He is tempted by simple pleasures. For instance, his accepting the dragon's egg is an extension of his need for companionship (which he finds through his "pets"—Fang, Fluffy, and Norbert). He is also tempted to overindulge in drinking.	Often he does not even realize that temptation has gotten the best of him. Once he realizes what he has done, however, he does everything in his power to solve the problems he has caused.
Ron	He is tempted to seek revenge (especially where Hermione is concerned). He is also tempted to give in to his fear.	His attempts at revenge backfire (like the incident with the slugs), and this teaches him the futility of impulsive vengeance. Ron is also an example of true courage. He is afraid, but overcomes his fear to serve a greater good.
Hermione	Her greatest temptation is found in her pride. She has a tendency to be arrogant and condescending. She is also tempted to lie to get out of trouble.	As the story progresses, she begins to understand the need for humility, and her arrogance is tempered with compassion.

Questions for Discussion

- After discussing the chart, have group members talk about their own struggles with temptation. With which characters do they most identify?

- Have a member of the group read the quote in which Dumbledore describes the power of the Mirror of Erised to Harry. The Mirror of Erised is the central symbol for temptation in the Harry Potter stories. What does Harry's encounter with the mirror have to say about the nature of temptation? (Harry is almost lost in the allure of what the mirror shows him. Almost always our greatest temptation is an extension of our greatest vulnerability. Harry wants so desperately to recover the lost love of his family that he is willing to give up everything else for even the illusion that he might be able to have it. Dumbledore allows Harry to struggle with his temptation because he knows that it is only in overcoming his weaknesses that Harry can find true strength [Paul discusses this in 2 Corinthians 11:30–12:10].)

- Have a member of the group read the story of the temptation of Christ as found in Luke 4:1–13. Does Harry face a similar temptation? (On at least two occasions Harry is faced with the temptation to accept the selfish ends of worldly power. The first is when he dons the Sorting Hat. The hat nearly places him in Slytherin, but Harry realizes the danger inherent in that possibility and wills himself away from the temptation. The second is when Voldemort offers Harry the chance to join him in the quest for absolute worldly power and immortality. Again, Harry understands the danger [and futility] that comes with the selfish pursuit of personal power.)

- Have a member of your group read James 1:12–16. According to James, what is the root source of temptation? (The passage says that "one is tempted by one's own desire, being lured and enticed by it." The parallel to the lesson Harry learns through his experience with the Mirror of Erised should be clear.)

- How does James suggest that temptation can be overcome? (Through faith, endurance, and perseverance in God's love.)

- According to James, what are the consequences of allowing our temptation to overcome us? (James says that "when that desire has conceived, it gives birth to sin, and that sin, when it is fully grown, gives birth to death." Your group should immediately see the connection between the consequences stated here and Voldemort.)

- Have a member of the group read Psalm 10:3–6. Does the psalmist agree with the writer of James? (Yes, he does. However, the psalmist takes it one step further. No one can escape being accountable to God. The wicked, says the psalmist, are so self-centered that they believe themselves to be outside the reach of God's judgment.)

- In the Harry Potter stories, how do relationships help individuals deal with temptation? (Harry and his friends show us that the love we have for one another helps us to hold one another accountable and supports us when we fail.)

Prayer: Our loving Creator, we realize that we would not need your grace if we were strong enough to always overcome our temptations. Help us to learn from our weaknesses and, by overcoming them, find new strength in your love. Help us to use that newfound strength to avoid temptation in the future. Amen.

Something to Talk About: Challenge the members of your group to find someone whom they trust in order to discuss the temptations they face. What temptations are the strongest? Do they have suggestions for dealing with temptation? How have they been able to overcome temptation? Have them share what they have learned with the group at your next meeting.

Six

Breaking Free from Slavery to Sin

Supplementary Reading: Harry, Ron, and Hermione's Soft Landing (pp. 36–38), Hagrid's Remorse (pp. 43–45), Introduction to Book Two (pp. 53–55), Mr. Weasley's Loophole in Magical Law (pp. 56–59), The Rescue of Ginny Weasley (pp. 80–82), and Dobby's Sock and Other Tales of Redemption (pp. 85–88) from *The Gospel according to Harry Potter*.

Useful Scenes from the Films: Scene 2 (Dobby's Warning), Scene 16 (No Longer Safe), Scene 25 (Cornelius Fudge), Scene 35 (Dobby's Reward), and Scene 36 (Welcome Back) in *Harry Potter and the Chamber of Secrets*.

Old Testament Scripture Lesson (Psalm 51:4–17): Against you, you alone, have I sinned, and done what is evil in your sight, so that you are justified in your sentence and blameless when you pass judgment. Indeed, I was born guilty, a sinner when my mother conceived me. You desire truth in the inward being; therefore teach me wisdom in my secret heart. Purge me with hyssop, and I shall be clean; wash me, and I shall be whiter than snow. Let me hear joy and gladness; let the bones that you have crushed rejoice. Hide your face from my sins, and blot out all my iniquities.

Create in me a clean heart, O God, and put a new and right spirit within me. Do not cast me away from your presence, and do not take your holy spirit from me. Restore to me the joy of your salvation, and sustain in me a willing spirit.

Then I will teach transgressors your ways, and sinners will return to you. Deliver me from bloodshed, O God, O God of my salvation, and my tongue will sing aloud of your deliverance.

O Lord, open my lips, and my mouth will declare your praise. For you have no delight in sacrifice; if I were to give a burnt offering, you would not be pleased. The sacrifice acceptable to God is a broken spirit; a broken and contrite heart, O God, you will not despise.

New Testament Scripture Lessons (Romans 7:14–8:1): For we know that the law is spiritual; but I am of the flesh, sold into slavery under sin. I do not understand my own actions. For I do not do what I want, but I do the very thing I hate. Now if I do what I do not want, I agree that the law is good. But in fact it is no longer I that do it, but sin that dwells within me. For I know that nothing good dwells within me, that is, in my flesh. I can will what is right, but I cannot do it. For I do not do the good I want, but the evil I do not want is what I do. Now if I do what I do not want, it is no longer I that do it, but sin that dwells within me.

So I find it to be a law that when I want to do what is good, evil lies close at hand. For I delight in the law of God in my inmost self, but I see in my members another law at war with the law of my mind, making me captive to the law of sin that dwells in my members. Wretched man that I am! Who will rescue me from this body of death? Thanks be to God through Jesus Christ our Lord!

So then, with my mind I am a slave to the law of God, but with my flesh I am a slave to the law of sin.

There is therefore now no condemnation for those who are in Christ Jesus.

(Romans 6:11–23): So you also must consider yourselves dead to sin and alive to God in Christ Jesus.

Therefore, do not let sin exercise dominion in your mortal bodies, to make you obey their passions. No longer present your members to sin as instruments of wickedness, but present yourselves to God as those who have been brought from death to life, and present your members to God as instruments of righteousness. For sin will have no dominion over you, since you are not under law but under grace.

What then? Should we sin because we are not under law but under grace? By no means! Do you not know that if you present yourselves to anyone as obedient slaves, you are slaves of the one whom you obey, either of sin, which leads to death, or of obedience, which leads to righteousness? But thanks be to God that you, having once been slaves of sin, have become obedient from the heart to the form of teaching to which you were entrusted, and that you, having been set free from sin, have become slaves of righteousness. I am speaking in human terms because of your natural limitations. For just as you once presented your members as slaves to impurity and to greater and greater iniquity, so now present your members as slaves to righteousness for sanctification.

When you were slaves of sin, you were free in regard to righteousness. So what advantage did you then get from the things of which you now are ashamed? The end of those things is death. But now that you have been freed from sin and enslaved to God, the advantage you get is sanctification. The end is eternal life. For the wages of sin is death, but the free gift of God is eternal life in Christ Jesus our Lord.

(John 8:33–36): They answered him, "We are descendants of Abraham and have never been slaves to anyone. What do you mean by saying, 'You will be made free'?"

Jesus answered them, "Very truly, I tell you, everyone who commits sin is a slave to sin. The slave does not have a permanent place in the household; the son has a place there forever. So if the Son makes you free, you will be free indeed."

Questions for Discussion

- Have a member of the group read Romans 7:14–8:1. What does Paul have to say about the nature of sin? (Paul speaks of a conflict between the flesh and the Spirit. Left to themselves, human beings are not capable of doing good and resisting evil because they are "sold into slavery under sin." Paul talks about doing what is right, but finds himself unable to do it. To make matters worse, the evil that he wants to avoid is what he ends up doing. The only way to break this cycle is to accept the grace of Jesus Christ.)

• Do you see what Paul is talking about being illustrated in the characters from the Harry Potter stories? (Just about every character in these stories is conflicted in his or her inner being. Harry battles the temptation to turn to the dark side and embrace evil; he sees that conflict acted out in his daily life. Hagrid has a checkered history and apparently has made some serious mistakes for which he wishes to be redeemed. Hermione battles her pride. Ron struggles with his impulsive tendency to act before he thinks. Each character seems to have his or her own version of the inner conflict of which Paul speaks being acted out in his or her life.)

• What about Dumbledore and Voldemort? How do they fit into all this? (Dumbledore and Voldemort are the exceptions when it comes to this intense inner struggle between flesh and Spirit. Dumbledore apparently has managed to overcome the tempta-tion to do or be evil in favor a life immersed in the power of love and goodness. Dumbledore could be seen as a symbol of a life lived in grace. It is not that this conflict has never been pres-ent in his life; it is just that he seems to have been able to over-come it. Voldemort, on the other hand, has given himself over completely to the flesh and is in a state of "slavery under sin." He wants absolute power and immortality and will go to any ends to achieve this. Voldemort has no desire to be anything other than what he has become. His whole life is completely focused on attaining more power.)

• Have a member of your group read Romans 6:11–23. This is the famous passage that ends with "For the wages of sin is death." How does this apply to Voldemort? (For all intents and purposes, Voldemort is already dead. In the first two stories he struggles to break free of a nether world in which he exists between life and death. He is dead to all the good things that bring happiness and joy into human existence. In fact, he seeks to destroy anything that reminds him that there might be another way to look at the world. He is, in effect, the living embodiment of Paul's idea that slavery to sin leads to death.)

• Have a member of your group read Psalm 51:4–17. Explain that this is a prayer David wrote after committing the horrible sin of sending Bathsheba's husband, Uriah, to die at the front lines so that David could have Bathsheba for himself. How does David deal with the conflict in his inner nature? (Even though he is an Old Testament figure, David follows all the steps necessary to receive God's grace and be forgiven. He admits that he has sinned [confession]. He acknowledges that God is justified in passing judgment on him [submission]. He asks for God's help to change [repentance]. He surrenders his ego and will to the awesome nature of God's power [obedience]. And finally, he vows to serve God and avoid sin in the future [renewal].)

• What do you think David means when he says, "The sacrifice acceptable to God is a broken spirit; a broken and contrite heart, O God, you will not despise"? (In order to be in right relationship to God we must come to the point in our lives when we realize that we are totally dependent on God's grace in order to be saved. David humbles himself ["a broken spirit"] and opens himself completely to God's Spirit ["a broken and contrite heart"]. Once David offers his brokenness to God, God is able to make him whole through grace.)

• Do you think Voldemort is irredeemable? (No Christian should ever consider any individual as irredeemable or beyond the reach of God's love and grace. If Voldemort were to turn from evil and follow the steps David followed in his prayer from Psalm 51, even he could receive God's grace.)

• Have a member of your group read John 8:33–36. Can the story of Dobby the house-elf be seen as a metaphor for enslavement to sin and saving grace? (Dobby's story is like a perfect little parable describing the way God's grace works in our lives. Dobby is enslaved. There is nothing he can do through his own power to break free from that slavery. Like Paul, he is unable to do the good things he wishes to do, and ends up assisting in evil actions which he despises. He wants to do good [his attempts to aid and protect Harry], but in the end is still a slave. He realizes when he makes mistakes and even punishes himself for them [Dobby inflicts pain on himself whenever he fails]. His own efforts to do penance and change are never effective in bringing about a real transformation in his life. The only thing that can break him from his slavery is the free gift of grace [symbolized by the gift of the sock]. Dobby could not "earn" his freedom from slavery, but was released from bondage by an unmerited gift of grace.)

Prayer: Our gracious and loving God, we realize that we have sinned before you and fallen short of what you expect from us. We find it hard to do the good we wish to do, and often end up doing the very thing we hate. We know that we deserve any judgment you would pass on us. We are completely dependent on you to bring change into our lives. Help us to turn back to you, open our hearts, and accept your loving forgiveness so that we can serve you in the world as witnesses to the transforming power of your grace.

Something to Talk About: During the week ahead, have the members of your group talk to friends, family, and other members of your spiritual community about the way that grace has transformed their lives. Have them answer the following questions: What was your life like before you realized or received God's grace? What brought about the change? How has God been working to help you mature in God's grace?

Dobby and Onesimus

If you are ever looking for a good single-session Bible study, then Paul's little letter to Philemon might be just the ticket. Most likely written just before Paul's death during his house arrest in Rome (A.D. 61–63), it is the most intimate and personal of Paul's many letters. Paul writes to Philemon on behalf of Onesimus, a runaway slave. Paul implores Philemon to receive Onesimus back without the severe punishment that runaway slaves would normally receive. Paul speaks of Onesimus having become like a son to him and compliments him on how valuable he has been to Paul's ministry. He reminds Philemon that since Onesimus has become a Christian he is no longer a slave but a brother in Christ. While Paul never directly mentions it, the undercurrent of the letter is a subtle suggestion that Onesimus be set free.

This in and of itself would be intriguing enough, but many scholars have suggested that the story gets even better. In the second century, Ignatius of Antioch wrote a letter to the church at Ephesus. In it he gives exceptional praise to the leadership of a bishop named (you guessed it!) Onesimus. He admonishes the Christians at Ephesus to live so as to be worthy of so wonderful a bishop. In his letter to Philemon, Paul puns on Onesimus's name, which in Greek means "useful." Scholars have pointed out that Ignatius of Antioch uses the very same pun when referring to Bishop Onesimus. It is almost as if Paul had given Onesimus a nickname. This seems to be a vital link between the two stories. If the two are the same, then Philemon set Onesimus free and he became one of the most revered leaders of the Christian church in his time. The parallels to the story of Dobby the house-elf should make for a fascinating comparison and stimulating discussion.

Seven

How Do We Overcome Prejudice?

Supplementary Reading: Diagon Alley: First Stop, Gringotts (pp. 17–18), Introduction to Book Two (pp. 53–55), and Pure-Bloods, Muggles, and Mudbloods (pp. 67–69) from *The Gospel according to Harry Potter*.

Possible Film Scenes: Scene 11 (Welcome to Hogwarts) in *Harry Potter and the Sorcerer's Stone*. Scene 12 (Mudbloods and Murmurs), Scene 13 (Writing on the Wall), and Scene 35 (Dobby's Reward) in *Harry Potter and the Chamber of Secrets*.

Old Testament Scripture Lesson (Deuteronomy 10:17–19): For the LORD your God is God of gods and Lord of lords, the great God, mighty and awesome, who is not partial and takes no bribe, who executes justice for the orphan and the widow, and who loves the strangers, providing them food and clothing. You shall also love the stranger, for you were strangers in the land of Egypt.

New Testament Scripture Lesson (Galatians 3:28): There is no longer Jew or Greek, there is no longer slave or free, there is no longer male and female; for all of you are one in Christ Jesus.

Activity: Have the definitions on page 42 written out on a marker board or newsprint but covered so the group will not be able to see or read at first. Ask the group what immediately comes to mind when you say the words *racist* and *bigot:* What does it mean

---

Some Definitions

Prejudice   The result of judging in advance or judging and determining before a cause is heard.

Racialism   The misguided belief that certain races are superior and pure while others are inferior or impure, which results in hatred or discrimination directed at the perceived inferior race.

Racism   The systematic practice of discrimination, segregation, persecution, oppression, and/or domination, based on perceived racial differences.

Racist   A person who believes, advocates, or practices racism.

Bigotry   Narrow-minded, intolerant attachment to a particular misguided belief or prejudice.

Bigot   A narrow-minded person who clings blindly and intolerantly to a particular misguided belief or prejudice.

---

to be a racist? Is being a bigot the same or different? Be sure to record their suggestions and comments. Have the group members work together to create their own definitions of the terms *racist* and *bigot*. After they are finished, reveal the dictionary definitions and discuss them. How are your group's definitions similar to the dictionary definitions? How are they different? Follow the same process in order to define Muggle, Mudblood, and pure-blood as they are used in the Harry Potter stories.

Questions for Discussion

- What are some of the examples of racism and bigotry in the Harry Potter stories? (Your group should immediately pick up on Malfoy's racial slur directed at Hermione. In fact, many members of Slytherin House are racist [evidenced by the fact that their password is "pure-blood"]. Draco Malfoy is also dis-

---

Some *Harry Potter* Definitions

Muggle   A nonwizard; a human being who is not capable of performing the art of magic.

Mudblood   A racial slur to describe any wizard of Muggle descent.

Pure-blood   Someone whose parents were both wizards who themselves had descended from wizards.

Half-blood   Someone who has one Muggle parent and one wizard parent.

Squib   Someone born into a family of wizards, but without magical powers.

---

dainful of people from a lower socioeconomic class [the Weasleys, for instance]. Still another example would be the way that Dobby is treated. See our examples listed on p. 44.)

- Why do you think that Draco Malfoy is prejudiced against Mudbloods? (Most prejudice and racism has its foundations in fear and insecurity. People are often afraid of anything different. Other people are raised with the idea that some people are superior to other people and therefore should be treated differently. For some people this is an issue of self-esteem. In order to feel good about themselves they look down on others. Draco Malfoy's problems are a combination of these factors.)

- Have someone read the quote in which Ron is discussing Malfoy's racial slur with Hagrid, Harry, and Hermione. What is Ron's perspective on this? (Ron finds it difficult to understand why someone would call another person a name that is intended to hurt that person. He has been raised to treat others as equals and not to prejudge or intentionally hurt others.)

- Have a member of your group read the quote from Harry's introduction to Draco Malfoy. How does Harry deal with this

"No one asked your opinion, you filthy little Mudblood."

—Draco Malfoy to Hermione Granger

"It's about the most insulting thing he could think of," gasped Ron, coming back up. "Mudblood's a really foul name for someone who is Muggle-born—you know, non-magic parents. There are some wizards . . . who think they're better than everyone else because they're what people call pure-blood." He gave a small burp, and a single slug fell into his outstretched hand. He threw it into the basin and continued, "I mean, the rest of us know it doesn't make any difference at all. . . ."

"It's a disgusting thing to call someone," said Ron, wiping his sweaty brow with a shaking hand. "Dirty blood, see. Common blood. It's ridiculous. Most wizards these days are half-blood anyway. If we hadn't married Muggles we'd've died out."

—Ron discussing Malfoy's racial slur with Hagrid, Harry, and Hermione

Excerpted from *Harry Potter and the Chamber of Secrets,* by J. K. Rowling (New York: Scholastic Press, 1999)

Draco Malfoy: It's true then, what they're saying on the train. . . . Harry Potter has come to Hogwarts. This is Crabbe, and Goyle, and I'm Malfoy. . . . Draco Malfoy.

(Ron sniggers)

Draco: Think my name is funny do you? No need to ask yours. Red hair, and a hand-me-down robe. You *must* be a Weasley. You'll soon learn that some wizarding families are better than others, Potter, and you don't want to go making friends with the wrong sort. . . . I can help you there.

Harry: I think I can tell the wrong sort for myself, thanks.

—Harry's introduction to Draco Malfoy, from the film *Harry Potter and the Sorcerer's Stone* issue? (When Malfoy suggests that Harry should be more discerning about the people with whom he becomes friends, Harry makes it clear that he can make those kinds of decisions for himself and will not prejudge anyone.

- Why do you think Harry is so accepting and tolerant? (One answer might be that he is just that way by nature. Another might be that he has put up with so much discrimination at the hands of the Dursley family that he understands how hurtful it can be. When Tom Riddle [Voldemort] tries to convince Harry to become his ally, he notes the similarities between them as "outsiders": They are both half-bloods, they are both orphans, they were both raised by Muggles, and they are both Parselmouths. It is Harry's status as an outsider that has prepared him to be tolerant and accepting of others. And although Harry is incredibly tolerant and accepting, even he gets accused of bigotry. At one point, Filch, the Hogwarts caretaker, accuses Harry of harming his cat [Mrs. Norris] because Harry has discovered that Filch is a squib. Of course, the accusation is untrue.)

- Have a member of your group read Galatians 3:28. What is the biblical standard for dealing with our differences? (Christians should not recognize differences, per James 2:1. In God's love we all have the same value. Making distinctions between people divides and separates. Christians are called to be inclusive and to value all people as part of the body of Christ.)

- Have a member of your group read Deuteronomy 10:17–19. What is the Old Testament standard for dealing with sojourners, strangers, and those who are less fortunate? (Because God is not partial, we should not be partial. It also commands the people of Israel to love the stranger because they had been strangers in Egypt. The Jews were despised and treated as slaves during the time they were in Egypt. God could give the Israelites no better illustration on how to deal with this issue than that.)

Prayer: Our loving Creator, everything in earth and heaven has been created by your loving hand. We know that you show no partiality. Help us to be truly tolerant and accepting of others. Guide us as we seek to find new ways to be inclusive and bring more people into the embrace of your loving grace. Give us the strength to fight racism, bigotry, and injustice wherever we encounter them. Amen.

Something to Talk About: Have the members of your group find someone in your family of faith who may have had experiences with intolerance, racism, or bigotry. Have them ask the following questions: How did it make you feel? How did you deal with it? Do you have any suggestions about how it can be dealt with?

Eight

What Should a Christian Think about Ghosts?

Useful Scenes from the Films: Scene 13 (Nick and Other Residents) in *Harry Potter and the Sorcerer's Stone*. Scene 17 (Dueling), Scene 22 (The Diary), Scene 29 (Chamber of Secrets), and Scene 36 (Welcome Back) in *Harry Potter and the Chamber of Secrets.*

Old Testament Scripture Lesson (Isaiah 8:19–20): Now if people say to you, "Consult the ghosts and the familiar spirits that chirp and mutter; should not a people consult their gods, the dead on behalf of the living, for teaching and for instruction?" Surely, those who speak like this will have no dawn!

New Testament Scripture Lesson (Luke 24:37–39): While they were talking about this, Jesus himself stood among them and said to them, "Peace be with you." They were startled and terrified, and thought that they were seeing a ghost. He said to them, "Why are you frightened, and why do doubts arise in your hearts? Look at my hands and my feet; see that it is I myself. Touch me and see; for a ghost does not have flesh and bones as you see that I have."

Activity: Assign different members of your group to read each of the six texts under the heading "Scripture Texts That Mention Ghosts." Discuss each one individually. What does it say about

Scripture Texts That Mention Ghosts

- Deuteronomy 18:9–14 (The people of Israel are warned against the abhorrent practices of the nations surrounding them, including the consulting of ghosts or spirits.)

- Isaiah 8:18–22 (Isaiah warns against any advice to "consult the ghosts and the familiar spirits" or "the dead on behalf of the living" and suggests that those who do will be in darkness rather than light. Note that this warning directly precedes the traditional Christmas lesson from Isaiah.)

- Isaiah 19:2–4 (Isaiah speaks of the Egyptians consulting "idols and the spirits of the dead and the ghosts and the familiar spirits.")

- Isaiah 29:4 (Isaiah warns that if God passes judgment, then the voice of Israel will "come from the ground like the voice of a ghost.")

- Matthew 14:22–34 and Mark 6:46–51 (When the disciples see Jesus walking toward them on the water, they first think that he is a ghost.)

- Luke 24:36–39 (When the disciples encounter the resurrected Christ, they again first think that he is a ghost.)

ghosts? To whom is it directed? What does it tell us about what the people of the Old Testament and of Jesus' time believed about ghosts?

Questions for Discussion

- How do you feel about the idea of ghosts?

- Why do you think some people believe in ghosts? (Answers might include but not be limited to: the desire for tangible evidence of life after death; to personalize and explain our irrational fears or to give substance to our fears of the unknown.)

Hogwarts's Ghostly Residents

Ghosts figure prominently in the Harry Potter stories, and in recent interviews J. K. Rowling has intimated that they will play an even greater role in future stories. While there are a multitude of ghosts roaming the halls of Hogwarts, each of the four houses has its own special "resident ghost." Gryffindor has Nearly Headless Nick (a.k.a. Sir Nicholas de Mimsy-Porpington), Slytherin has the Bloody Baron (as of yet we do not know why he is bloody), Hufflepuff has the Fat Friar, and Ravenclaw has the Grey Lady (who, according to J. K. Rowling, makes an anonymous appearance in *Harry Potter and the Sorcerer's Stone*). Each of these four disembodied spirits more or less represents the essence of the students "sorted" to be part of the house in which they reside. Another prominent ectoplasmic entity is Peeves the Poltergeist (who has not yet appeared in the movies), who Nearly Headless Nick informs us is not really a ghost at all (a poltergeist is a "mischievous spirit" that you can blame for all those sounds that go bump in the night). Still, the ghost with the most and the star thus far has to be Moaning Myrtle, who takes center stage as a key part of the solution in *Harry Potter and the Chamber of Secrets*.

- From your discussion of "Scripture Texts That Mention Ghosts," it should be obvious that the people of the Old Testament and of Jesus' time believed in ghosts. How does that make you feel? (Note that these texts all assume that ghosts are real and that people can communicate with them in the actual, physical world. The prohibitions from the Old Testament are generally directed against practices that come to the Israelites from other religions.)

- Have a member of your group read Luke 24:36–39. How does Jesus deal with the disciples when they are fearful of his resurrected presence because they believe he is a ghost? (He first reassures them and then instructs them to confirm for themselves that he is not a ghost.)

- How does Jesus calm the disciples' fears and reassure them that what they are seeing is not a ghost but his resurrected presence? (He tells them to look at his hands and feet [the wounds that will tell them that he is the same Jesus who died for them on the cross]. He also challenges them: "Touch me and see; for a ghost does not have flesh and bones as you see that I have.")

- What functions do the ghosts in the Harry Potter stories serve? (To communicate clues that give Harry an advantage in his struggle against evil and to provide a connection to the past. Moaning Myrtle is an excellent example of this. It is a good bet that in the future, ghosts aligned with evil will begin aiding Voldemort and opposing Harry.)

- Do you think it is appropriate for Christians to believe in ghosts?

- Do you think that a Christian can read a fantasy novel that features ghosts as characters without it influencing his or her Christian values? (It would be important to stress here that the scriptural admonitions about ghosts are directed toward the belief that ghosts actually exist and can influence life and events in the real world.)

Prayer: O God, you are the source of every good thing we can experience. Sometimes, however, we are afraid. We know that you understand that being afraid is an expression of our human weakness. Help us to deal with our fears by centering ourselves in your love. Show us once again that true love casts out all fear. Amen.

Something to Talk About: Send your group out to talk with people they love and respect in regard to how they feel about the idea of ghosts. Why do people believe in ghosts? Is it appropriate for Christians to believe in ghosts? A natural extension of this discussion would include a conversation about fear and how it can be overcome.

Nine

Courage and Self-Sacrifice

Supplementary Reading: Why the Evil One Could Not Touch Harry (p. 48), A Last-Minute Change of Decorations (pp. 49–50), You've Got to Make Some Sacrifices (pp. 65–66), and A Songbird and an Old Hat (pp. 76–79) in *The Gospel according to Harry Potter.*

Useful Scenes from the Films: Scene 8 (The Boy Who Lived), Scene 18 (Mountain Troll), Scene 28 (Wizard's Chess), and Scene 29 (Sacrifice Play) in *Harry Potter and the Sorcerer's Stone.* Scene 30 (Backfire), Scene 31 (Heir of Slytherin), Scene 32 (The Basilisk), and Scene 33 (Healing Powers) in *Harry Potter and the Chamber of Secrets.*

Old Testament Scripture Lesson (Isaiah 53:3–8): He was despised and rejected by others; a man of suffering and acquainted with infirmity; and as one from whom others hide their faces he was despised, and we held him of no account.

Surely he has borne our infirmities and carried our diseases; yet we accounted him stricken, struck down by God, and afflicted. But he was wounded for our transgressions, crushed for our iniquities; upon him was the punishment that made us whole, and by his bruises we are healed. All we like sheep have gone astray; we have all turned to our own way, and the LORD has laid on him the iniquity of us all.

51

He was oppressed, and he was afflicted, yet he did not open his mouth; like a lamb that is led to the slaughter, and like a sheep that before its shearers is silent, so he did not open his mouth. By a perversion of justice he was taken away. Who could have imagined his future? For he was cut off from the land of the living, stricken for the transgression of my people.

New Testament Scripture Lessons (John 15:12–14): This is my commandment, that you love one another as I have loved you. No one has greater love than this, to lay down one's life for one's friends. You are my friends if you do what I command you.
(Matthew 2:16–18): When Herod saw that he had been tricked by the wise men, he was infuriated, and he sent and killed all the children in and around Bethlehem who were two years old or under, according to the time that he had learned from the wise men. Then was fulfilled what had been spoken through the prophet Jeremiah: "A voice was heard in Ramah, wailing and loud lamentation, Rachel weeping for her children; she refused to be consoled, because they are no more."
(Matthew 16:24–26): Then Jesus told his disciples, "If any want to become my followers, let them deny themselves and take up their cross and follow me. For those who want to save their life will lose it, and those who lose their life for my sake will find it. For what will it profit them if they gain the whole world but forfeit their life? Or what will they give in return for their life?"

Activity: Introduce your group to the idea of a Christ figure in books and movies. Have them discuss the ways in which Harry Potter can be seen as a Christ figure. Keep track of their responses, then compare them to those listed on page 57.

Questions for Discussion

- Have a member of your group read John 15:12–14. What are some examples of sacrificial love in the Harry Potter stories? (Answers should include but not be limited to: Both Harry's father and mother die to prevent Voldemort from killing him

"Don't be a fool," snarled the face. "Better save your own life and join me . . . or you'll meet the same end as your parents. . . . They died begging me for mercy. . . ."

"LIAR!" Harry shouted suddenly.

Quirrell was walking backward at him, so that Voldemort could still see him. The evil face was now smiling.

"How touching . . ." it hissed. "I always value bravery. . . . Yes, boy, your parents were brave. . . . I killed your father first, and he put up a courageous fight . . . but your mother needn't have died . . . she was trying to protect you. . . . Now give me the Stone, unless you want her to have died in vain."

> —Voldemort confronts Harry during the climactic battle in *Harry Potter and the Sorcerer's Stone*, by J. K. Rowling (New York: Scholastic Press, 1998)

when he is a baby. Harry and Ron give no thought to their own safety while battling the troll. Ron risks himself as a sacrifice in the wizard's chess game. Harry goes on to battle Voldemort alone in order to recover the Sorcerer's Stone. Nicolas Flamel destroys the Stone even though he knows it will mean his death. Harry battles the basilisk in order to save Ginny and defeat Riddle/Voldemort; in the process he is poisoned by the giant serpent's fang.)

- Why do you think both Harry's father and mother gave their lives for Harry? (Other than the fact that most parents would willingly sacrifice their lives to protect their children, there seems to be something much larger at work here. Have a member of your group read Matthew 2:16–18. Herod is so frightened of the potential power of the baby Jesus that he orders all the infants under two years of age killed to make sure Jesus does not live. It becomes obvious that there is something about Harry that makes him the key to the defeat of evil, and his parents must know this.)

Amy Hollingsworth, contributing writer at Crosswalk, gives a mother's testimony about encountering the movie with her son: "When my son and I exited the theatre . . . he didn't once mention an oppressive desire to worship Satan or to turn people to stone or to fly on broomsticks. His first remark (one he returned to again and again) was concerning the scene, depicted rather benignly by a flash of light, where Harry's mother is killed trying to save him, then a baby. My son didn't take away a fascination for the occult, only the thing that touched him the most: a young boy losing his mother. He noted the loss; I noted the sacrifice. Powerful images, heartfelt lessons—not the kind likely to be spawned from the loins of Beelzebub."

(From "Film Forum: Hobbits, Wizards, and Rappers" by Jeffrey Overstreet, *Christianity Today*, November 11, 2002. The original article may be accessed at http://www.christianitytoday.com/ct/2002/144/41.0.html.)

- How is the incident with the troll an example of sacrificial love? (First, Harry and Ron put themselves at risk in order to return and warn Hermione. When the troll goes after Hermione, Harry and Ron draw its attention away from her and put themselves in danger. Harry throws himself at the troll without thought to his own safety. After it is all over, Hermione takes the blame.)

- What about the sacrifice during the chess game? (The sacrifice in the chess game is a perfect symbol of sacrificial love. In chess it is often necessary to sacrifice one piece in order to gain an advantage that will allow another piece to win the game. In this case, Ron realizes that he must sacrifice himself if Harry is to win the game. Ron does this willingly even though it means he might be seriously harmed or even killed.)

- If Dumbledore is the most powerful wizard alive, why is it Harry who must risk everything and battle Voldemort alone?

(For some reason, Harry is the only person who is capable of taking on Voldemort one on one. We know that there is something about Harry that will eventually empower him to defeat Voldemort for good. Also, when Harry is recovering in the infirmary, Dumbledore tells him that only someone who would not be tempted to use the Sorcerer's Stone could actually recover it. Does Dumbledore realize that he would be tempted to use the Stone just as his friend and partner Nicolas Flamel had been using it all these years? Could it be that it is Harry's character and strength of will rather than his power as a wizard that will allow him to defeat Voldemort?)

- Have a member of the group read the quotation in which Voldemort confronts Harry during the climactic battle in *Harry Potter and the Sorcerer's Stone*. What is Harry's temptation during this struggle? (Once again Harry is tempted with absolute power and once again it is not an option he is willing to consider. Even when Voldemort offers him his heart's true desire [to bring his parents back] Harry does not waiver from the course of good for a second.)

- Have a member of the group read Matthew 16:24–26. How does this apply to the Harry Potter stories? (Jesus tells us that true sacrificial love takes no thought to its own self-interest or even the threat of physical death. As the resurrection demonstrates, death itself can be defeated.)

- Why is Nicolas Flamel's decision to destroy the Sorcerer's Stone a sacrificial act of love? (Flamel has kept himself alive all these years by using the power of the Stone. Even though he is able to control the Stone's power, he realizes that if it falls into the hands of Voldemort, Voldemort's power would be too great to defeat. Understanding this, Flamel destroys the Stone even though he realizes it will lead to his own death.)

- Have a member of your group read Isaiah 53:3–8. What does this have to say about the nature of sacrificial love? (This is one of the most famous messianic prophecies in the Bible. In it,

Isaiah tells us that the Messiah must suffer in order to accomplish his ultimate purpose, namely, to give human beings salvation through the free gift of grace. The suffering on the cross was necessary for the power of the resurrection to be alive in the world.)

Prayer: God of love and grace, we are eternally grateful for the gift of your son Jesus Christ. Without his great sacrifice of love in going to the cross, we would not have the grace that sustains us and saves us. Help us to reflect the power of that sacrificial love back into the world by living our lives as Jesus would have us live. Amen.

Something to Talk About: Have your group talk to friends and family about the times in their lives when sacrificial love played an important role. Have them ask the following questions: Has someone ever made a great sacrifice for you? Have you ever had to sacrifice for others? How did this change your life?

Is Harry Potter a Christ Figure?

A Christ figure is a character in a movie or a book that is symbolic of Jesus Christ. Often, it will be easy to spot a Christ figure, as he or she will strike a "crucifixion pose," with arms outstretched emulating Jesus on the cross. A sacrificial death on behalf of others is a clear sign, and sometimes there will even be a resurrection. Another way to spot a Christ figure is to see the ways events in his or her life parallel events in the life of Jesus. The symbolic Christ figure in a book or movie might perform miracles and healings, and he or she will most often have "followers" or "disciples." Is J. K. Rowling presenting Harry to us as a Christ figure? There are several indications in the first two books and movies that she is. Consider the following:

- Harry is spared from death when he is a baby. This parallels the "slaughter of the innocents" story found in Matthew 2:16.

- Harry's wand is made from the feather of a phoenix. The phoenix is a symbol of resurrection.

- Harry is tempted with great power on at least two occasions: when he dons the Sorting Hat and when he confronts Voldemort at the end of the first book and movie. This parallels the temptation of Jesus as found in Matthew 4:1–11, Mark 1:12–13, and Luke 4:1–13.

- Ron and Hermione, while part of Harry's team, function as his "followers" or "disciples."

- At the end of *Harry Potter and the Chamber of Secrets*, Harry's arm is pierced by the poisonous fang of the giant basilisk and it looks as though he will die. The tears of Fawkes, Dumbledore's phoenix, heal the wound and Harry does not die. Again, the phoenix is a symbol of resurrection.

- Almost everybody Harry encounters assumes that he will do some great thing. He seems destined to be the one who will defeat a great evil.

Ten

Good versus Evil:
The Oldest Conflict in Creation

Supplementary Reading: The Quest for the Sorcerer's Stone (pp. 33–35) and Harry's Battle with the Dark Lord (pp. 46–47) in *The Gospel according to Harry Potter.*

Useful Scenes from the Films: Scene 8 (The Boy Who Lived), Scene 19 (Quidditch), Scene 20 (Interference Overcome), Scene 30 (Man with Two Faces), and Scene 31 (Magic Touch) in *Harry Potter and the Sorcerer's Stone.* Scene 30 (Backfire), Scene 31 (Heir of Slytherin), Scene 32 (The Basilisk), and Scene 33 (Healing Powers) in *Harry Potter and the Chamber of Secrets.*

Old Testament Scripture Lesson (Genesis 3:1–6): Now the serpent was more crafty than any other wild animal that the LORD God had made. He said to the woman, "Did God say, 'You shall not eat from any tree in the garden'?" The woman said to the serpent, "We may eat of the fruit of the trees in the garden; but God said, 'You shall not eat of the fruit of the tree that is in the middle of the garden, nor shall you touch it, or you shall die.'" But the serpent said to the woman, "You will not die; for God knows that when you eat of it your eyes will be opened, and you will be like God, knowing good and evil." So when the woman saw that the tree was good for food, and that it was a delight to the eyes, and that the tree was to be desired to make one wise, she took of its fruit and ate; and she also gave some to her husband, who was with her, and he ate.

58

New Testament Scripture Lessons (Romans 5:12–19):
Therefore, just as sin came into the world through one man, and death came through sin, and so death spread to all because all have sinned—sin was indeed in the world before the law, but sin is not reckoned when there is no law. Yet death exercised dominion from Adam to Moses, even over those whose sins were not like the transgression of Adam, who is a type of the one who was to come.

But the free gift is not like the trespass. For if the many died through the one man's trespass, much more surely have the grace of God and the free gift in the grace of the one man, Jesus Christ, abounded for the many. And the free gift is not like the effect of the one man's sin. For the judgment following one trespass brought condemnation, but the free gift following many trespasses brings justification.

If, because of the one man's trespass, death exercised dominion through that one, much more surely will those who receive the abundance of grace and the free gift of righteousness exercise dominion in life through the one man, Jesus Christ.

Therefore just as one man's trespass led to condemnation for all, so one man's act of righteousness leads to justification and life for all. For just as by the one man's disobedience the many were made sinners, so by the one man's obedience the many will be made righteous.

(John 1:1–5): In the beginning was the Word,

> "After all, to the well-organized mind, death is but the next great adventure. You know, the Stone was really not such a wonderful thing. As much money and life as you could want! The two things most human beings would choose above all—the trouble is, humans do have a knack of choosing precisely those things that are worst for them."
>
> —Dumbledore to Harry, explaining why Nicolas Flamel chose to destroy the Sorcerer's Stone even though it meant his death.
>
> Excerpted from *Harry Potter and the Sorcerer's Stone*, by J. K. Rowling (New York: Scholastic Press, 1998)

and the Word was with God, and the Word was God. He was in the beginning with God. All things came into being through him, and without him not one thing came into being. What has come into being in him was life, and the life was the light of all people. The light shines in the darkness, and the darkness did not overcome it.

Questions for Discussion

- Have a member of your group read Genesis 3:1–6. How does the serpent convince Eve to eat the fruit from the forbidden tree? (He tempts her by saying, "When you eat of it your eyes will be opened, and you will be like God, knowing good and evil.")

- What is the consequence of her action? (God told Adam and Eve that if they ate from the tree, they would die. This would be a good place to reemphasize Romans 6:11–23.)

- Are there any parallels between the Harry Potter stories and the story of Eve's temptation? (The conflict between good and evil is as old as creation itself. Eve makes the first human decision to defy God by making the wrong choice. Voldemort believes he can have absolute power and live forever; this sounds like someone who wants to be "like God" [in French, *vol de mort* means "flight from death"]. On at least two occasions Voldemort offers Harry the same temptation. It is intriguing that Harry is a Parseltongue [he can can speak to serpents] and must slay the basilisk [a giant serpent] in order to defeat Voldemort and rescue Ginny Weasley in *Harry Potter and the Chamber of Secrets*. Also, the motto of Hogwarts school is *Draco dormiens nunquan titillandus*, which translates "Never tickle a sleeping dragon." Could this be another reference to that pesky serpent?)

- Have a member of your group read Romans 5:12–19. What does this verse tell us about the eternal struggle between good and evil? (Even though sin entered the world through the choice of Adam and Eve, grace also has entered the world through the choice Jesus made to go to the cross and die for our sins. God has given us the way to overcome sin by offering the free gift of grace in Jesus Christ.)

- Have someone from the group read John 1:1–5. What does the introduction to the Gospel of John have to say about this eternal struggle between good and evil? (The redeeming love of Jesus has been part of God's intention since before the world was created. Only Jesus gives us the power to overcome sin and death through the free gift of grace by his death on the cross. Because of this, the darkness can never overcome the light. Evil can never defeat good. Eventually good will triumph.)

Activity: Have a member of your group read each of the following quotes from J. K. Rowling, and then ask the group the questions listed below it.

1. "Children's books aren't textbooks. Their primary purpose isn't supposed to be 'Pick up this book and it will teach you this.' It's not how literature should be. You probably do learn something from every book you pick up, but it might be simply how to laugh. It doesn't have to be a slap-you-in-the-face moral every time. I do think the Harry Potter books are moral books, but I shudder to think that any child picking one up would get three chapters in and think, Oh, yeah, this is the lesson we're going to learn this time" (from an interview in *Newsweek*, July 1, 2000).

- Do you agree with what J. K. Rowling says here, or do you think that the Harry Potter stories are intended to teach us something?

- Do you agree that the Harry Potter stories are moral (that is, they clearly define the difference between right and wrong, good and evil)?

- Do you think that the primary purpose of the Harry Potter stories is to entertain us, and what we learn in the process is only secondary?

2. "I'm writing about shades of evil. You have Voldemort, a raging psychopath, devoid of the normal responses to human

suffering. . . . Then you have Wormtail [Voldemort's right-hand man], who out of cowardice will stand in the shadow of the strongest person. What's very important to me is when Dumbledore says that you have to choose between what is right and what is easy . . . because what is easy is often not right" (J. K. Rowling, quoted in Jeff Jensen, "Hocus Focus," *Entertainment Weekly*, August 11, 2000).

- What do you think Rowling means when she says she is writing about "shades of evil"? (Our character and principles are determined by our choices. People can choose to do the wrong thing, even something evil that hurts themselves or others, but that does not necessarily make them "completely" evil.)

- But what about a guy like Voldemort—isn't he "completely" evil? (In the Harry Potter stories, characters such as Voldemort had to *choose* to be as evil as they are. At one time, they were faced with the opportunity to choose the good. As they continued to make choices that led them deeper into selfishness, they became progressively more evil until they lost sight of the good. In Christianity, we can never believe that any person is irredeemable. We believe that grace can change anything. Sometimes, however, it is difficult for us to believe that someone as evil as Voldemort could ever change.)

- What does Rowling mean when she has Dumbledore say that we must "choose between what is right and what is easy . . . because what is easy is often not right"? (The choices that lead to evil are often the easiest to make. Once we begin to take the easy way out and make exceptions to our principles, we find that we no longer hold those principles. Christian principles are the foundation of what we are in God's love. If we compromise our Christian principles to take the easy way out, we betray everything that we profess to believe.)

3. "What I'm working towards here is the fact that our choices rather than our abilities show us what we truly are. That's brought out in the difference between Harry and his arch enemy, Tom Riddle. In *Chamber of Secrets*, Harry is told by the hat that if he

goes into Slytherin he will become a powerful wizard. He chooses not to do that. But Tom Riddle, who has been twisted by ambition and lack of love, succumbs to the desire for power. Though he's supposed to have died years before, his malign spirit manipulates events through an enchanted diary" (J. K. Rowling, from an interview in the *Sydney Morning Herald,* October 28, 2001).

- What does J. K. Rowling say is the difference between Harry and Tom Riddle? (When he is trying to convince Harry to join him, Tom Riddle goes to great lengths to show Harry how much they are alike. And it is true, their backgrounds are similar, their intellect is similar, and their abilities are similar. Each of them can build on what he has been given in order to have power. What makes them different is their choices. Harry chooses good; Tom chooses evil.)

- Do you agree that it is our choices and not our abilities that make us what we are?

Activity: In his article "Discerning the Presence of Christ at the Centre of Culture," Julian Jenkins of the Macquarie Christian Studies Institute has set up some criteria for discerning whether a book or film is ultimately helpful or hurtful to a Christian worldview. (Jenkins's complete article can be found at http://www.mcsi.edu.au/think/index.htm). You may want to read the article before leading the following activity.

A chart delineating "Qualities Leading away from Christ" and the corresponding "Qualities Leading toward Christ" can be found on page 65. A scale has been added across the top to help quantify the extent to which the category leads toward Christ or away from Christ. For instance, a rating of +3 for the category "Imparting Life" would mean that the story or film is exceptionally life affirming. A rating of +1 would mean that the story or film is only somewhat life affirming. The reverse would be true of the opposing category, "Demeaning Life." A rating of –3 would mean that the story or film is highly demeaning of life and a –1 would mean that the story or film is only somewhat demeaning of life. A rating of 0 would be neutral.

Have each member of your group individually rate the Harry Potter stories in each of the categories. Encourage them to work alone and not share their answers. After they have all finished, divide them into several smaller groups of four or five members each and have them share and discuss their ratings. Why did they rate each category the way they did? If there are differences, have

---

Resisting Evil: Professing Your Faith

Most denominations have a profession of faith that asks the person making the profession to renounce evil. Below is a sample of such a profession from the first Baptismal Covenant of the United Methodist Church:

"On behalf of the whole church, I ask you: Do you renounce the spiritual forces of wickedness, reject the evil powers of this world, and repent of your sin?" (The answer, of course, is "I do.")

The next question takes this a step further:

"Do you accept the freedom and power God gives you to resist evil, injustice, and oppression in whatever forms they present themselves?" (Again, the answer is "I do.")

Have your group do a little research in order to discover similar professions of faith in your denomination or tradition. What do these professions of faith have to say about the expectations of the community of faith when it comes to evil? Does the church believe that individual Christians are empowered to resist evil? Does the church believe that human beings have the freedom to choose evil over good? How does this correspond to J. K. Rowling's insistence that it is our choices, not our abilities, that make us what we truly are? Which of the characters in the Harry Potter stories would you expect to have made a profession like this one? Which characters would defy such a profession of faith?

Qualities Leading toward Christ				Qualities Leading away from Christ		
+3	+2	+1	0	-1	-2	-3
Imparting Life				Demeaning Life		
Uplifting the Soul				Destroying the Soul		
Awakening the Conscience				Deadening the Conscience		
Sharpening the Senses				Numbing the Senses		
Enlarging One's Being				Confining One's Being		
Reveling in Beauty				Reviling Beauty		
Revealing Truth				Concealing Truth		
Challenging Negative Stereotypes				Reinforcing Negative Stereotypes		
Eliciting Empathy				Fueling Antipathy		
Attacking Hypocrisy				Overlooking Hypocrisy		
Reconciling Offenses				Proliferating Offenses		
Exposing the Effects of Sin				Distorting the Effects of Sin		
Providing Consolation				Producing Desolation		
Inspiring Awe				Engendering Boredom		
Instilling Hope				Disarming Hope		
Upholding Grace				Affirming Greed		
Embodying Love				Empowering Lust		

them discuss the reasons for these differences. Once the small groups have finished sharing, bring the whole group back together to discuss what each small group discovered.

Prayer: O God, you are the source of all goodness and true power. We know that the world is full of deception and evil, and we depend on you to help us to discern the direction we should take. Help us to always choose what Jesus Christ would have us do. Help us to always choose you.

Something to Talk About: Have members of your group find other members of your family of faith who have read the Harry Potter stories or seen the movies. Using the context of what they have learned through the session in this study, have them listen to what other people have to say about this incredible phenomenon. The only way we can understand each other as Christians is to talk to one another about what we believe without judging one another.

Index of Scenes from the Films
Harry Potter and the Sorcerer's Stone and
Harry Potter and the Chamber of Secrets

Harry Potter and the Sorcerer's Stone

DVD (Scene as listed in the Movie Scene Index)	VHS (Approximate VCR counter time from the first appearance of the Warner Brothers logo in Hours: Minutes:Seconds format)
1. Doorstep Delivery	0:00:30
2. Vanishing Glass	0:06:20
3. Letters from No One	0:08:50
4. Keeper of the Keys	0:13:40
5. Diagon Alley	0:18:50
6. Gringotts	0:22:15
7. Ollivanders	0:25:00
8. The Boy Who Lived	0:29:20
9. Platform 9 3/4	0:31:30
10. Ron and Hermione	0:34:30
11. Welcome to Hogwarts	0:38:10
12. Sorting Hat	0:41:45
13. Nick and Other Residents	0:47:00
14. Potions and Parcels	0:51:00
15. New Seeker	0:55:30
16. Three-headed Sentinel	1:01:30

17. Facts and Feathers	1:06:30
18. Mountain Troll	1:08:30
19. Quidditch	1:15:50
20. Interference Overcome	1:20:30
21. Christmas Gift	1:25:30
22. Cloaked in Darkness	1:28:30
23. Mirror of Erised	1:32:30
24. Norbert	1:39:00
25. Forbidden Forest	1:43:30
26. Up to Something	1:46:30
27. Through the Trapdoor	1:51:30
28. Wizard's Chess	2:01:00
29. Sacrifice Play	2:04:00
30. Man with Two Faces	2:07:00
31. Magic Touch	2:12:30
32. Mark of Love	2:14:30
33. House Cup Winner	2:17:45
34. Not Really Going Home	2:22:00

Harry Potter and the Chamber of Secrets

DVD (Scene as listed in the Movie Scene Index)	Video (Approximate VCR counter time from the first appearance of the Warner Brothers logo in Hours: Minutes:Seconds format)
1. In a Cage	0:00:30
2. Dobby's Warning	0:03:15
3. Car Rescue	0:08:10
4. The Burrow	0:11:00
5. To Diagon Alley	0:14:20
6. Flourish and Blotts	0:18:10
7. Flying to Hogwarts	0:22:20
8. Whomping Willow	0:26:00
9. Not Expelled . . . Today	0:29:00

10. Mandrakes; Ron's Howler 0:31:25
11. Gilderoy Lockhart 0:35:30
12. Mudbloods and Murmurs 0:38:10
13. Writing on the Wall 0:42:55
14. About the Chamber 0:48:25
15. Rogue Bludger 0:52:25
16. No Longer Safe 0:58:05
17. Dueling Club 1:02:45
18. A Parselmouth 1:08:00
19. Nothing to Tell 1:12:05
20. Polyjuice Potion 1:17:30
21. Harry and Ron Transformed 1:21:40
22. The Diary 1:25:45
23. Tom Riddle 1:29:50
24. Petrified 1:33:35
25. Cornelius Fudge 1:37:50
26. Aragog 1:42:55
27. Spider Attack 1:47:05
28. Missing 1:51:10
29. Chamber of Secrets 1:55:30
30. Backfire 2:00:55
31. Heir of Slytherin 2:04:15
32. The Basilisk 2:09:35
33. Healing Powers 2:14:35
34. Out of the Hat 2:18:05
35. Dobby's Reward 2:21:30
36. Welcome Back 2:26:35